W H E N

A Book of Poetry

By

Shirley S. Watkins

Copyright © 2013 Shirley Watkins

Published by Around H.I.M. Publishing
For publishing information, address:

Around His Image Marketing and Publishing
5 W. Hargett Street
Raleigh, NC 27601
info@aroundHim.com

All rights reserved, including the right of reproduction in whole or in part in any form.

No part of this publication may be stored in any retrieval system or transmitted in any form or by electronic, mechanical, photocopying, recording or otherwise without the written permission of the publisher except the case of brief quotations embodied in critical articles and reviews.

Manufactured & printed in the
United States of America

ISBN-13: 978-0615859842

"For I know the thoughts that I think toward you, saith the LORD, thoughts of peace, and not of evil, to give you an expected end."

Jeremiah 29:11 (KJV)

A MESSAGE TO THE READERS:

- *You are not alone. We all have been at a point in our lives where we have asked God "when".*

- *What I hope to accomplish in this book is to reach someone; in other words, to be a fisher of both men and women!*

For speaking engagements and more information about this author contact:

(919) 345-4370
(919) 985-3631

<u>W</u>ait

<u>H</u>ope

<u>E</u>ndure

<u>N</u>ever give up

To believers and non-believers everywhere.

"Through wisdom is an house builded; and by understanding it is established:"

Proverbs 24:3

I would say, when Lord, when, when, when and He would say at the appointed time.

"For the vision is yet for an appointed time, but at the end it shall speak, and not lie: though it tarry, wait for it; because it will surely come, it will not tarry."

Habakkuk 2:3

I know you have been going through. I know it's been hard, but many are the afflictions of the righteous (Ps 34:19) and the Lord wants you to know that He hears when the righteous cry. (Ps 34:17). The Lord's desire is that you hold on and hold tight because your due season is coming.

Galatians 6:9

TABLE OF CONTENTS

Chapter 1 "Oh Taste And See"
- Poem 1 2
- Poem 2 4
- Poem 3 6
- Poem 4 8
- Poem 5 10

Chapter 2 "I Know My Thoughts"
- Poem 1 13
- Poem 2 15
- Poem 3 17
- Poem 4 19
- Poem 5 21

Chapter 3 "A Changed Life"
- Poem 1 24
- Poem 2 26
- Poem 3 28
- Poem 4 30
- Poem 5 32

Chapter 4 "Lord, Perfect Me"
- Poem 1 35
- Poem 2 37
- Poem 3 39
- Poem 4 41
- Poem 5 43

Chapter 5 "Wonderfully And Fearfully Made"

Poem 1 46

Poem 2 48

Poem 3 50

Poem 4 52

Chapter 6 "Holy Ghost, The Promise"

Poem 1 57

Poem 2 59

Poem 3 61

Poem 4 63

Chapter 7 "Be Still"

Poem 1 68

Poem 2 70

Poem 3 72

Poem 4 74

Be Still 76

Poem 5 76

Chapter 8 "Watching And Waiting"

Poem 1 79

Poem 2 81

Poem 3 83

Poem 4 85

Poem 5 87

CHAPTER 1
"Oh Taste and See"

Scripture References

Psalms 32	Psalms 27
Psalms 33	Romans 8
Exodus 14	Daniel 6
Daniel 7	Amos 4
Psalms 31	Psalms 37
Psalms 145	Luke 11
Luke 12	Acts 8
Proverbs 10	Revelations 21
Proverbs 11	Amos 5
John 10	2 Corinthians 5
Romans 6	Matthew 22
Romans 12	Psalms 108
Psalms 34	

Oh Taste and See

POEM 1

Taste and see that the Lord is good.

He will forgive your sins like He said He would.

You are my hiding place….only after you, Lord, will I chase.

I will sing of your goodness

Yes, I will sing a new song

It was because of our sins that He was hung

He divided the waters, yes, He parted the Red Sea

He did it for Israel, for you and He did it for me.

Our Ancient of Days, sitting on His chair

Listening, answering and blessing every prayer.

Oh Lord, instruct and teach me in the way I should go,

Yes I believe you will watch over me and give me good counsel -- for your Word says so.

When my eyes grew weak from sorrow,

WHEN

You gave me hope for tomorrow.

When I was in distress,

It was you who gave me rest.

When grief clothed my body and soul,

You still helped me to reach my goal.

I can trust in you like I knew I should,

You brought me out, I just knew you would

Oh Taste and See…

Oh Taste and See

POEM 2

Do not worry about your food --your daily bread,

Know that God is faithful and in His Word, He said

Do not worry about your life, what you will eat

Or about your body, what you will wear

He says I am your Heavenly Father and yes, I do care.

The Lord will not let the righteous go hungry, now wouldn't you agree,

The blessings of the Lord brings prosperity and wealth

He gives us many benefits and good health

I'm grateful that my mind is not double

For our God will rescue the righteous from trouble.

Oh taste and see that the Lord is good

He will bring you out like He said He would

WHEN

The Lord is our Good Shepherd; He laid down His life for the sheep and

You can trust in Him, *your* soul He will also keep.

Serving God is good, the benefits you shall reap,

It will lead to holiness and the result is an eternal life.

God grooms the church to make her His wife

Therefore I urge you to offer your body as a living sacrifice.

Come on, do it today, don't think twice and certainly, don't delay

Oh taste and see that the Lord is good.

Oh Taste and See

POEM 3

My soul will boast of your love for me, and

I will cry out and tell how you made me free.

Though my father and my mother may forsake me, my God will take me in.

He will teach me His ways and forgive me all my sins,

God will cause all things to work for the good

So, come on and serve Him, you really should.

Predestined, called, justified and glorified

You'll have so much to look forward to once you've been tried.

Nothing can separate us from His love

God has His eyes on us from above.

He rescued Daniel from the lion's mouth; He will save in the east, west, north and south.

For He rescues and He saves and yes he performs signs and wonders, it's true

WHEN

He did it for me and He'll do it for you.

When times got hard, you were there, my King

So to you I will lift my voice and sing

You who forms the mountains and creates the wind

You who forgive all men their sin

I'm so glad that you are my God and I am your child

I'm glad I've been forgiven, so now I can smile.

Thank you Jesus!

Oh Taste and See

POEM 4

Your favor for the meek will cause them to inherit the land and enjoy great peace.

Your love for mankind will not cease.

The wicked plot against the righteous, but the Lord laughs at them.

That's why we cannot afford to let our shining light go dim.

The Spirit Himself testifies with our spirit that we are God's children,

I'm glad the Lord prayed for us that we would not grow wild.

For the sinful mind is death, but the Spirit controlled mind is life, peace and yes, good health.

You held back the rain, delivered me from pain.

You healed the paralyzed, crippled and sick, you healed a grieving heart with love….and no tricks.

Oh, what a great God we serve my friend try God your heart he will mend.

WHEN

He will wipe all tears from your eyes; He did it for me when I would cry.

So seek Him my friend and live

A new life to you He will certainly give.

The old has gone, the new has come

Many are called but He has only chosen some.

His love is higher than the heavens, and His faithfulness reaches to the sky

He will forgive you and receive you. Just give Him a try.

Praise the Lord!

Oh Taste and See

POEM 5

You heard my cry for mercy and my call for help you heard,

I'm so grateful that you are true to your Word.

My weeping may remain all night but

Joy will come in the morning light.

As you walk with me hand in hand

Lord, continue to keep me from the evil man

Help me not to fret nor be envious over those who do wrong.

But teach me to pray and sing to you a new song.

You help David slay Goliath its true

You'll help me overcome my enemies too.

All who touched Jesus was healed

He made them free and they were thrilled.

In the shelter of your presence you hide them

WHEN

You'll heal us all like the woman who touched your hem.

Lord you watched over me day and night

You made sure that everything was alright.

The voice of the Lord is majestic and powerful too

The voice of the Lord is over the waters for the God of Glory thunders its true.

Blessed are the meek and those who morn,

  Even to those which are torn.

Ask and it will be given to you, seek and you will find

We are salt and light and God wants us to shine.

God Bless You!

CHAPTER 2
"I Know My Thoughts"

Scripture References

Jeremiah 29	Lamentations 3
Jeremiah 30	Isaiah 57
Jeremiah 31	Psalm 30
Psalm 32	Joel 2
Joshua 1	Matthew 22
Nehemiah 9	Proverbs 8
Matthew 7	Ephesians 6
Jeremiah 33	Romans 8
Isaiah 61	Hosea 13
Isaiah 56	Isaiah 55
Philippians 4	2 Kings 20
Lamentations 2	

I Know My Thoughts

POEM 1

I know my plans; they are deeper than any ordinary man.

See I come to prosper and not to harm

You can trust me; come rest in my arms

You will find me when you seek me with all your heart

There will be nothing no one could say or do to tear us apart

You see I have a future plan that will bring great hope

So put up your wine and let go of your dope.

For I am the Lord God who loves thee

I gave my son to set you free.

I will give a listening ear

When you come and pray; I will draw ever so near

Seek and you shall find me

For I am your Father and I shall always be

SHIRLEY WATKINS

For I am that I am…

…And I know my thoughts

I Know My Thoughts

POEM 2

I will rebuild your dwelling place

For I am your God and I will take on your case

I have loved you with an everlasting love

And drawn you with loving kindness

And no longer will you have to tolerate your enemies' mess.

The plans of the Lord stand firm forever

God will not leave you, no not ever.

Blessed be your glorious name.

I'm so glad for me you came.

Because of you, I can stand tall

Let your name be exalted above all.

The covenant I made with Israel is sure

The words I put in their hearts are pure

I put my law in their mind.

I told them to seek and they would find

Call to me and I will answer you and tell you great

And unsearchable things you do not know.

For I sit high, but I've been below.

I will heal my people and will let them enjoy the abundance of peace and security.

For I have come to set the captives free.

Maintain justice and do what is right, for my salvation is close at hand.

For in my image I made man

So seek the Lord while He may be found.

And He will place your feet on solid ground.

WHEN

I Know My Thoughts

POEM 3

The days are coming when my people shall recover their land

For this has always been my original plan

I will heal your wounds and restore your health

I will supply your every need and give you great wealth

For I've heard your prayers and seen your tears

I've been watching over you for many many years

Many eyes fail from weeping

Because my commandments you were not keeping

Children and infants falling out in the street

Some fell faint for lack of water and meat.

Some in their mother's arms looking for bread and wine

Some retreat to hiding where no one could find

Yet this I call to mind, that God has been kind.

Because of His great love, we are not consumed, therefore

I have hope

For His compassions never fail

He will fight for you and your enemies will not prevail

For your faith is greater than your hurt

So wipe away the tears from your eyes and tuck in your shirt

For great is God's faithfulness.

Amen!

I Know My Thoughts

POEM 4

I will satisfy you my child with abundance,

My love for **you Father** is like a hot romance.

I will refresh the weary and satisfy the faint

I will clean you up and call you my saint.

I will guide you and restore

I will protect you for evermore

You said our weeping may endure for a night

But joy would come in the morning

You said you will repay what the locusts have eaten up, this is true

All we have to do is to return to you

Just mourn, weep and fast

And you will bring it to pass.

I will pour out my spirit on all flesh, you know

It's for my glory –not a show.

I will use your sons and daughters and bring their youth alive with zeal

I will cause them to prophesy and show them I am real.

For the appointed time has come

I've called many, and have chosen some

Love the Lord your God with all your heart, soul and mind

Seek Him and you will find

Love your neighbor as your self

Obey your parents and receive long life and good health

For with God is riches, honor, prosperity and enduring wealth

For God's thoughts and ways are higher than mine

So I will let Him lead and I will follow close behind.

For God is good.

I Know My Thoughts

POEM 5

Hear the Word of the Lord O' nations and sorrow

No more for new wine and oil

For I shall take care of you and nothing will spoil.

I will give you comfort and joy

You will feel like a child with a brand new toy.

Some call you an outcast for whom no one seem to care

But I will heal your wounds and carry what you cannot bear,

I will remember your afflictions and bitterness of heart

I will deliver you and give you a fresh new start.

Let us lift up our hearts and our hands to God in heaven and say

It is you Oh Lord, who I chose to obey.

For we have called from the depths of our soul

And it is you who have made us whole.

When I called you – you came near

You touched my body and said do not fear.

For you have remembered us in our times of need

You have taken care of us and our seed.

You have caused things to work together for our good

Just like you said you would.

You cared for us in the desert heat

You made sure we had enough to eat

For I am the Lord your God and there is no other

So tell your sister and tell your brother

For I AM ……..and I know my thoughts.

Chapter 3
"A Changed Life"

Scripture References

John 3	Romans 7
Romans 8	Romans 10
Matthew 5	Matthew 6
Matthew 7	Matthew 8
Matthew 9	Mark 2

SHIRLEY WATKINS

A Changed Life

POEM 1

The good that I would, I do not

Until Jesus came and took Satan's spot

What the law could not do

God gave His son, yes, that's true

For flesh obey flesh spirit obey spirit

Did you hear it? A changed life

Bought with a price

Had a heart cold as ice

Carnal minded equals death

Spiritual minded equals life and peace.

I wrote this so that your faith would increase

You must be born again

Come to God, He'll forgive your sin

So confess Jesus with your mouth

Believe God hath raised Him from the dead in your heart

WHEN

God did all of this to give you a brand new start.

A changed life, no longer the same

I'm so glad Jesus changed my name

Hallelujah, Hallelujah, Hallelujah

I have been changed.

A Changed Life

POEM 2

Brand new mercies each and every day

For the former things are passed away

Look unto Jesus, the author and finisher of our faith

Give Him your life, please madam --please sir

He promised no more death, no more sorrow

Aren't you glad He is our hope for tomorrow?

He feeds the fowls of the air

He clothes the grass of the field

To leave us out is not part of the deal.

You see, we're known by the fruits we bear

That's why this Gospel I indeed must share.

Jesus will change your life

Not only yours --but your husband and your wife.

Birds have nest and foxes have holes,

Jesus is the answer for your soul

Try Jesus! He'll make it better, He'll comfort you

And see you through

I'm telling you His Word is true.

He will be right there because He loves you and He really cares.

A changed life!

A Changed Life

POEM 3

Lay aside every weight and sin

My sister, my brother, let Jesus in.

He will make all things new

He did it for me, He'll do it for you.

I use to sing a sad story

Now I sing He's the King of Glory

This old bottle cannot hold new wine

Serving Jesus is no crime

The light of the body is the eye

When I think of His goodness it makes me want to cry

Trying to serve two masters leaves your life in total disaster

Take no thought for your life, give it to Jesus, please, don't even think twice

Now we are the salt of the earth and the light to the world.

WHEN

I'm so happy I'm one changed girl.

I use to worry about tomorrow, but I found out, He'll take away my sorrow did not know what I would wear or eat.

But I learned to cast that at Jesus feet.

Yes, a changed life.

A Changed Life

POEM 4

Cast all your cares upon Him spiritual, physical, mental, emotional (yes)

He wants all of them.

You will understand it better by and by

Come to the rock that's higher than I

Jesus will take your cares away

He went to prepare a place for you to stay

He will give you a new song to sing

Just give it to Him, that's right, give Him everything.

Give Jesus your heart; He'll give you a fresh start

The sins of the past; leave them there

Your present and future, God wants to share

Because He lives you can face tomorrow

He wants to give you joy in place of sorrow

All that you have been through

WHEN

God was with you

Standing with arms open wide

Waiting for you to say, come in side.

A changed life.

A Changed Life

POEM 5

The bible is true, so don't be surprised

When God wipes all tears from your eyes --He is our superstar

Call on Him

He's not far.

He's the lifter up of my head

It's because of Him we're not dead

Say no to crack

God has your back

Let go of drugs

Stop being a thug

Put down your beer

Jesus is on His way here

A changed life, don't think twice

Fall on your knees today

Look to heaven and say

WHEN

Father forgive me of all my sins

Into my heart Jesus come in

I want to live for you today

I don't care what family and friends will say

Jesus I want to go back with you one day

Here are my troubles --I cast them away

Fill me with your Holy Spirit

These words I speak, Jesus please hear it.

A changed life

Thank you Jesus

Thank you Jesus

Yes, indeed, a changed life.

Chapter 4
"Lord, Perfect Me"

Scripture References

Psalm 138	1 Peter 2
Hebrews 12	James 5
Isaiah 6	Hebrews 13
Proverbs 4	Isaiah 1
Psalm 15	Proverbs 6
Psalm 17	Psalm 80
Job 1	Psalm 81
Psalm 6	James 3
Psalm 11	Proverbs 1
Mark 5	Proverbs 3
Luke 11	Psalm 8
Song of Solomon 6	Job 14
Song of Solomon 7	

Lord, Perfect Me

POEM 1

O Lord, to look at me, one would trip

For I am a man of unclean lips

Please touch my mouth and take away my guilt

Unless inside my spirit will wilt

For I was nothing, less than a worm

But now for you Lord, my heart doeth burn

Be merciful to me, Lord, for I am faint

Continue to work on me Lord, and make me your saint

Perfect me so in your sanctuary I may dwell

Perfect me so I will not lift my eyes in hell

Probe my heart and examine me at night

Fix me dear Lord, and make me right.

Help me dear Lord, not to slip

For of your cup I do sip

O Lord save me by your hand

Cause me to become a righteous man

Like Job, blameless and upright

Work on me Lord, even if it takes all night

Naked I came from my mother's womb and naked I will depart

But I am asking you, dear Lord, work on my heart.

Lord, perfect me.

Lord, Perfect Me

POEM 2

Lord, you are the author and finisher of our faith, this is true

I'm so glad to be numbered among your crew.

Hear, O Lord, my righteous plea

Touch my eyes so I might see.

Lord I realize you observe the sons of men

To shield, protect and deliver from sin

It's with your eyes you examine them

To be made whole I'll touch your hem.

Make me so others will be drawn to your light

Use me dear Lord throughout the day and throughout the night

Cleanse me inside and out –just like a dish or cup

Make me holy so with you and the Father I can sup.

Help me, dear Lord, to love every man

Help me! Help me! I know you can.

For the unbeliever you are the stone that causes men to stumble and a rock that makes them fall

Help us dear Lord, not to be like Saul.

For we are Holy, Royal and Chosen

Deliver us from the unsaved and frozen.

Elijah was a man who prayed that it would not rain

Deliver us dear Lord from all of our pain.

For we praise you, with the fruit of our lips

For from your cup we have sipped.

Lord, perfect me!

Amen

Lord, Perfect Me

POEM 3

My God, take me wash me and make me clean

Take away my evil, so I will not be mean

Come now, let us reason together the Lord has spoke

For upon those words I did choke.

Who me, you would forgive you who would rebuke

death and cause me to live.

My sins like scarlet, but you will make white as snow.

For it was you who took the keys from Satan below

It was you my Lord who told me not to forsake

My mother's teaching and to keep my father's commands

It was you who told me to place everything in your hand

I was fed with the bread of tears; I had to drink my tears by the bowlful for many years

Restore Oh Lord and make your face shine upon me again

Keep me close, dear Lord, so I won't sin

Lord, perfect me, even in your rebuke that I will not perish

It's your wisdom and knowledge that I do cherish

It was you who fed me with the finest wheat

It is you dear Lord who sits in the highest seat.

Restore Me

Lord, Perfect Me

POEM 4

Lord you said if I keep my mind on you, you would keep me in perfect peace

You said your love for me would never cease

Help us not to harbor bitterness, envy, nor hate

Help us dear lord to lighten our plate

Teach us Lord to do what is right, just and fair

As we pour out our hearts you showed how much you care

You did not reject me when I would call, but you taught me how to stand tall

You taught me how not to ignore you but to take your advice, However after one rebuke I didn't think twice.

When I was overwhelmed with trouble and distress

You were the one who cleaned up my mess

For your Word declares that whoever listens to me will live

In safety and be at ease, without fear of harm

For it was in the hard places when you carried me in your arms.

Help me Lord to keep your commands in my heart,

Help me not to forget your teachings less my life would fall apart.

Let your love and faithfulness never leave me

Take a hold of my eyes so I can see.

I want to win your favor and obtain a good name

I want to tell the world how my life has truly been changed, since in to it you came.

Lord, perfect me.

Lord, Perfect Me

POEM 5

To appear like the dawn, bright as the sun and fair as the moon

Just to think our Lord will be here soon.

Work on us dear Lord, with your craft man's hand

Continue to keep us on safe and dry land

O Lord, Our Lord, how majestic is your name

I'm so glad to earth for me you came.

Thank you for wisdom because long life is in her right hand

She causes me to do right in the sight of God and man.

Those who lay hold of her will be blessed

You won't have to worry about every day's stress.

Lord, by wisdom you laid earth's foundation and by understanding you set heaven in place

Lord, perfect me this is my case.

For you give grace to the humble, but fools you put to shame

Teach us your ways Lord for this is no game.

We do not want to envy a violent man nor choose any of his ways

Lord, we understand that a man born of a woman is but a few days

If we listen to you Lord, when we run, we will not stumble

If we listen our dreams will not crumble.

Show us how to put away perversity from our mouth

And corrupt talk far from our lips

Give us dear Lord just a few tips

Although Lord, sometimes your words are bitter as gall

Help us dear Lord to receive them all.

God Bless You!

Chapter 5
"Wonderfully and Fearfully Made"

Scripture References

Psalm 138	Proverbs 11
Genesis 1	Proverbs 12
II Corinthians 5	Romans 6
Romans 8	Matthew 15
Lamentations 3	Psalm 144
Psalm 85	Galatians 5
Genesis 2	Matthew 4
Proverbs 10	

SHIRLEY WATKINS

Wonderfully and Fearfully Made

POEM 1

O Lord, what is man that for him you care

With him your beautiful heaven you want to share

Why do you think about the Son of Man?

Is it because you formed him by your hand?

His face, his eyes and his hair

His nose and mouth, you put them all there

Your smile, my smile, It took Him a while

The frame of your body, fingers and toes

Some freckles, some bare skin and even some moles.

Let us lift up our hearts and hands

To the One in heaven who understands.

Although days come and days go

It seems as if time moves so very slow.

WHEN

Skin white, brown, yellow or black

God will not leave you in lack because He is not slack

Hair blonde, black or brown

God will never let you down.

Although we look different and our thoughts are too

Big or small, God love us one and all.

And His love is true

We can be happy, although very different

We are made by the same hand

Because that's the way God's mastered His plan

Yes, we are wonderfully and fearfully made.

Blessings to you!

Wonderfully and Fearfully Made

POEM 2

God formed man from the dust of the ground,

It's because of man, God still hangs around.

Man does not live by bread alone,

He lives because God still sits on the throne.

God caused man o be a living being,

I know for some, believing is seeing.

From the ground, deep and dark,

God formed man from His heart.

Now the fear of the Lord adds length to life

From man's rib comes Eve, his wife.

You see a man of understanding holds his tongue

It is God who chastises him, especially when he's wrong.

A gossip betrays a confidence

WHEN

Lord, when will this ever make some kind of sense?

An evil man is trapped by his sinful talk

Too proud to apologize, so man just takes a walk.

A righteous man escapes his troubles, because you, dear Lord, gives him double.

The way of a fool seems right to him,

Not knowing that his light has gone dim.

A wise man listens to advice,

He considers the matter and he thinks twice.

Because he realizes that he has been wonderfully and fearfully made.

God bless you!

Wonderfully and Fearfully Made

POEM 3

Your love for man, O Lord, is mighty and strong

that all night you could hold him in your arm.

Just to think, you would part your heavens and come down

I can trust your words, not one will fall to the ground.

Love and faithfulness meet together, hand in hand,

Righteousness and peace kiss each other.

It was you dear Lord who taught me how to pray for my brother

Do you get it?

He wants us to live in the spirit.

Wonderfully and fearfully made by your hand

It was you Almighty who made man.

In man you placed the spirit of love

WHEN

All your goodness comes from above.

You gave man the spirit of joy

You grew him up from a young boy.

You placed in him the spirit of peace

You caused all his storms to cease.

You gave him patience through his test

You encouraged him to run with the best.

In man you put kindness

You cleaned him up with your goodness

You gave man the spirit of gentleness and self control

Because you gave man faithfulness he can now stand bold.

To God Be the Glory!

Wonderfully and Fearfully Made

POEM 4

When I consider your heavens, the work of your fingers,

I have to cast down doubt so in my mind it will not linger.

What is man that you are mindful of him and you give to him a place to dwell?

You sent your only son to keep man from Hell.

What is man that you would feed four thousand strong?

With seven loaves of bread and a few small fish

What is man that you are listening, hearing every prayer; to answer everyone's wish?

What is man that you would deliver the blind, crippled, and the lame --

Not to mention the mute and the insane.

Clothed like the clouds, shining like the sun

WHEN

It's all because of what the Lord has done.

He has made my skin and flesh at a ripe age **grow** (old)

When I call Him, He never places me on hold.

God's compassions never fail, His love is precious, hard to find

Yes our Lord is one of a kind.

He has made your face and my face

He made all the human race.

He has made some short and some tall

I'm not kidding, He made us all.

You accept me, I accept you

It's all because of God, now that's true.

How sweet it is!

Yes, we are wonderfully and fearfully made.

Wonderfully and Fearfully Made – Poem 5

Man was created in the image of God our Father

Who made the heaven and earth,

It was by Him that we have new birth.

What we are in God's eye is plain

It's because of Him we are not insane.

An eternal house not built by human hands

But by the same one who created the seas and the dry land.

We are a new creation, the old has long gone,

Who are you to throw that stone.

We have been reconciled now and we are ambassadors,

Sin has no power over us anymore.

For Christ has given us power to deal with our struggle with sin,

It's up to us to let Him in.

Once we receive Him, we become His child,

We are no longer left alone to grow rugged and wild.

To the orphans and homeless, you now have a Father who cares,

Once you receive Him, Heaven he will share.

WHEN

For you were wonderfully and fearfully made

Your adoption papers signed in blood will never fade.

This was created by God, out of love

This was completely filled with His spirit from up above.

Abba Father, will go with us all the way,

For it's because of Him we can have this day.

Amen!

Chapter 6
"Holy Ghost, the Promise"

Scripture References

Acts 1	John 14
Genesis 1	John 15
Acts 2	John 16
Mark 1	Ephesians 1
Romans 8	John 3
II Peter 1	Luke 24
1 Corinthians 2	1 Corinthians 14
II Corinthians 1	1 John 2

Holy Ghost, the Promise

POEM 1

Having made known unto us the mystery of His will,

After ye have heard the Word of Truth, the Gospel of your salvation that the Holy Spirit of Promise was sealed.

John baptized with water, but ye with the Holy Ghost

Not many days --go tell it from coast to coast.

When the Holy Ghost comes on you, you will receive power

When Jesus returns, no man knows the day or the hour.

On the day of Pentecost, the spirit of God moved in the upper room,

He is still moving in our life today so that we will not be doomed.

Suddenly in the room a sound blowing as a violent rushing wind,

Jesus knocking at the door of your heart, won't you let Him in?

Resting on them in the upper room were tongues of fire,

You filled with the Holy Ghost is my desire.

I pray you receive the spirit of wisdom and revelation

If you ask, God will give it to you without hesitation.

God bless you!

Holy Ghost, the Promise

POEM 2

Apostles stay in Jerusalem and wait for the promise,

Do not become like doubting Thomas

Ye shall receive power after the Holy Ghost is come upon you

The words that I speak they are true

Over the waters, the spirit of God hovered in the beginning

He's on the scene to keep you from sinning.

The Holy Ghost is your light,

He is the one to guide you through the night.

The promise is for you and your children, but that's not all,

For the promise is for the far off and for all whom the Lord will call.

Did you hear it?

Christ will forgive you your sins and fill you with the Holy Spirit

Thank you Lord, for the Holy Ghost has made a difference in my life,

And I tell you, if I knew then what I know now I would have not thought twice.

For those who stand in awe and not in doubt,

Thank you for pouring your spirit out.

Holy Ghost, the promise from the Father above,

He descended on Jesus like a dove.

The Holy Ghost came.

That you and I WOULD NOT remain the same.

Thank you Jesus!

Holy Ghost, the Promise

POEM 3

Although I'm going to leave you, do not cry

The Father is going to clothe you with power from on high

You will do well to listen to the prophet's word as to a light shining in a dark place

For men spoke from God as they were carried along by the Holy Spirit in and out of space

The Holy Ghost like the wind cannot be controlled or contained

He'll show you the Father's love and take away your pain.

For you have received the spirit of Sonship

His spirit leads us to love and to draw --not to trip.

His spirit helps us in our weakness

He'll help us get things off our chest.

The spirit Himself intercedes for us when we do not know what to pray

He leads us and guides us and gives us what to say.

We groan and make sounds that words cannot express

He helps us and keeps us through our test.

The spirit of God searches our hearts if we let him He'll do His part

For the saints the spirit intercedes, I'm so glad I'm God's seed.

The Holy Spirit helps us to line up with God's will, that's enough to give me a chill.

Being led by the promised Holy Ghost is a good thing

Love, joy and peace to your life He will bring.

With Christ's spirit you can over come

You can overcome all things not just some.

So thank God for His spirit from on high

For with His spirit we will understand it all, better by and by.

Holy Ghost, the Promise

POEM 4

We will do greater works because of the Holy Ghost power

We will blossom and bloom like a beautiful flower.

No longer ignorant, we have been trained by the best

He has cleaned us up better than Zest.

We now have divine wisdom and divine life

God's Word has cut us worst than the sharpest knife.

The promised Holy Ghost has given us a sound mind

Because we have received Him, we will not be left behind.

I'm so thankful for God's manifested glory

For without Him I could not tell my story.

Jesus said that He was going away

However He would send the Holy Ghost to us to stay.

Our Counselor, the Spirit of Truth, Jesus said he would testy of me

He will dwell in your so all can see.

1st - With the Holy Spirit hidden things are revealed

2nd - With the Holy Spirit, sick people are healed

Our Comforter in the morning, noon and night,

He is our Comforter to make all things right.

The promised Holy Ghost whom the Father sent in Jesus' name,

Will lead, guide and teach us all things without fame.

Grace and peace be multiplied unto thee!

Holy Ghost, the Promise – Poem 5

Because of Christ's Spirit there is no condemnation

He'll help you to escape all of your temptations.

What the eye has not seen, nor the ear has heard, the Spirit of God has revealed

Yes God's secret wisdom was hidden and it has been sealed.

Because of God's promised Spirit, the secrets of your heart will be laid bare.

God will balance the scale and make His judgments fair.

We have an anointing from the Holy One, you know;

Indeed it's because of Him that we will **grow and grow and grow.**

The Holy Spirit protects our salvation and our future plan

So come on, put your life in God's hand.

God will clothe you with His Spirit that will cause demons to flee,

I'm speaking from experience, because He did it for me.

In us is a power so great, I want you to know, God made no mistake

The promised Holy Spirit breathes upon the slain

It's for the good of us he came.

He breathes upon the dry bones and causes them to live,

He breathes upon man's heart and causes him to give.

The promised Holy Ghost makes what is weak, strong

If you trust in Him, He won't lead you wrong.

The promised Holy Ghost will bring you into a place of deliverance, like no other,

I plead with you, to give Him a chance, my sister and my brother.

The Promise!

Chapter 7
"Be Still"

Scripture References

Psalm 23	Psalm 26
Psalm 46	John 8
Psalm 47	Psalm 31
3 John	Psalm 25
Gen 1	Matthew 11
Psalm 37	Psalm 89
Psalm 90	Proverbs 3
Psalm 62	Psalm 27
Isaiah 1	Psalm 1
Psalm 24	

SHIRLEY WATKINS

<u>Be Still</u>

POEM 1

Be still and know that I am God

I'm a present help in the time of storm

I'll be with you to keep you from harm

Believe on me, I'll set you free

Like the river beside the tree

Be still.

Be still my child, be still

For I'm the Lord God and yes I'm real

So clap your hands and shout for joy

For I am the Lord of Lords, and King of Kings

My people shall not want for anything

I'm your shepherd and my pastures are green

So go ahead, lie down my child, lie down and be still

Your soul I shall restore

So walk with me and you'll want for no more

Be still my child, be still.

Be Still

POEM 2

Be still and hold to that which is good,

Be loving, kind and gentle as a good Christian should.

Be fruitful, be prosperous, and be in good health

Go on, enjoy life; enjoy your wealth.

Enjoy safe pasture, dwell in the land

Remember God can do what no man can.

You do not have to fret because of evil men,

God avenged you once, and He'll do it again.

Be still and trust in the One who calms the raging seas,

Trust the One who listens as you drop to your knees.

The One who's arm is endued with all power,

The One you can call upon, each and every hour.

Be still, for the Lord is our dwelling place,

WHEN

He'll never leave you in this Christian race.

For a thousand years are as one day

Just trust God and it will be okay.

Your barns will be filled to an over flow,

Set your mind on things above and not on things here below.

Be still, be still my child, be still and wait on Him; be still.

Be Still

POEM 3

My soul finds rest in God alone,

For it is He who sits upon the throne

He is our rock and our salvation

It was He who formed the world, and all of its creation.

Find rest my soul and rest in Him

Read His Word; don't let your light go dim.

Be still my soul do not be shaken,

One day with Him, we will be taken.

God will make us glad for many, many days

Let's trust Him and acknowledge Him in all our ways

He is our defense, so you say peace be still

God is the One who will carry us over the hill.

Trust not in oppression, but trust in God

WHEN

For our God has spoken and what He said shall come to pass.

Be still my soul and rest in God

He will lead you to a pasture filled with beautiful green grass.

There He will restore your soul,

Oh, yes my friend, He will make you whole.

So do not fear the evil man,

  because Jehovah our King has a greater plan.

Be still!

Be Still

POEM 4

Be still and wait, I say upon the Lord

He will wash you, clean you and take away your filthy rags

He will forgive your sin, take you in and with open arms He will welcome you in.

Be still like the tree planted by streams of water

Not like the leaf the wind blows away.

Delight in the law of the Lord and meditate therein day and night,

He will gently take your life and make it all right.

Be still my soul, the Lord is on your side

Come to the light, for you no longer have to hide.

The earth is the Lord's, and the fullness thereof belongs to Him,

So rest in it and do not be moved by *them*.

Lift up your head for our God is alive –no, He's not dead

WHEN

1st – Go tell your family and friends what Jehovah Word has said

2nd - Let *them* know His Word will not allow you to be ashamed.

That at any time of day you have the right, to call upon His Holy name.

Be still.

Be Still

POEM 5

Come unto me for my yoke is easy and my burdens are light,

Come on, rest my child, just sit tight.

Hear my voice and please, be still

Don't be afraid, yes I am for real.

Walk in God's integrity and let Him examine your heart,

God will show you His love and kindness --don't let Satan tear you apart.

But be still and listen to the voice of our Heavenly Father

Go right ahead, call Him --it's no bother.

Put down your watermelon and set aside your tea,

Go on and call upon God, He will make you free.

All day, all night, talk to Him; He will make everything all right.

Oh how great is thy goodness which thou hast laid up for them that fear thee,

Even to those who were once blind, but now they see

Oh, love the Lord, all ye His saints and be still.

Let the Lord have your battles he'll fight them, for real.

You just trust in Him and please, BE STILL.

Chapter 8
"Watching and Waiting"

Scripture References

John 14	Luke 21
Luke 12	Luke 17
1 Corinthians 4	Proverbs 8
Matthew 26	Matthew 24
1 Thessalonians 4	Mark 13

Watching and Waiting

POEM 1

Standing at the doorway, waiting for my Lord's return,

I'm looking to heaven -- because I do not want to burn.

Take heed that you are not deceived, for many will come in my name,

They will say he's over here and he's over there; they will try to convince you that Christ came.

The Lord will have you to watch and pray

Tell me, could you not watch one hour? Say.

The spirit is willing, but the flesh is weak

The more you believe the more you will seek.

There will be wars and rumors of wars, nations against nations and even famines and earthquakes in the land.

At the appearing of these fearful events, you my child must stand.

Be dressed and ready and keep your lamps trimmed and burning

Be watchful for our Lord is returning.

Be watching and be waiting until He comes again

Go tell your brothers, go tell your friends

I want you to be sober in the end.

Be on watch and please be alert, I don't want your feelings hurt.

Waiting can be a hard thing to do,

But while you wait, here's a clue

Fast and pray, day and night

So when He comes, you will be all right.

Watching and waiting.

Watching and Waiting

POEM 2

For the day or hour our Lord will return, no one knows, not even the angels nor the Son,

Not even the souls that have been won.

The Son of Man said the days will be like those of Noah, people marrying, given in marriage, eating and drinking.

People doing all sorts of things – not even thinking.

So it was the same in the days of Lot, gee, I know that made our enemies hot.

People eating and drinking, buying and selling

Some planting, some building where they are dwelling.

When all of a sudden out of heaven, fire and sulfur came

Since then nothing has been the same.

So as you are watching and waiting, don't forget to pray

SHIRLEY WATKINS

I don't care what anyone else may say.

You pray and stand your watch, and be on guard, keep looking out,

1st – Must I scream, yell and shout.

2nd - Jesus is drawing ever so near, there's no time for you to fear.

One left one taken, after the heavens and earth are shaken.

No time to look back, no time to be slack.

No time to sleep, no time to creep.

No time to doubt, no time to fall out.

Get yourself together and watch.

Amen!

Watching and Waiting

POEM 3

As the stars fall from the sky and the heavenly bodies be shaken

As you look around the elect will be taken.

Once the sun becomes darkened and the moon gives no light, and to some, that will be a fright.

Here comes the son of Man on the clouds

No more sorrows no more trials.

There he is up in the sky with great glory and power

Be sure to keep watch for no man knows the hour

Those who are asleep he will gather first

To tell this makes me want to burst.

To meet the Lord in the air, this will be such **great joy**

I'm sharing this with you, please choose not to ignore,

girl or boy.

Caught up together those still alive

We're in store for a wonderful ride.

The Lord Himself coming from heaven with a loud command

I'm looking forward to being in His holy band.

There it is the voice of the archangel

The trumpet call of God

Thank you, dear Lord, for guiding me with your rod.

Forever with the Lord, encourage one another.

God bless you!

Watching and Waiting

POEM 4

Here I am watching daily at my door,

I'm sipping from your Word, until I can't take no more.

For there is an appointed time for your return,

when the day or the hour, no one can discern.

The Lord will come at an hour when you do not expect Him

So be sure to witness and tell all of them.

Tell them Christ came but He will come again

It's time for you to let go of your sin.

For He will bring to light what is hidden in darkness

1st – He will deliver you from your mess.

2nd - He will expose the motives of men's hearts

And give to each brand new starts.

And if by chance you fall asleep at camp

SHIRLEY WATKINS

Be sure to rise and trim your lamp.

For here the bridegroom come, He came for many but only found some

So while all awake from sleep and some fetch oil the bridegroom will arrive.

What a great time to be alive

Alive to attend the Lord's wedding banquet

Living life with no regrets.

All of a sudden the door was shut

Knock, knock, knock I don't know you those words we don't want to hear

So make sure you're watching and waiting for the Lord is drawing near.

Watching and Waiting

POEM 5

What I say to you I say to all

Don't let anyone make you fall.

Brother will betray brother, a father his child.

That's enough to drive anyone wild.

Children will rebel against their mom and dad

Yes, those days will be very sad.

We will be hated because of our stand for Christ to the end

But we will be saved from that man of sin.

I can only wonder Lord when; when will this be over and behind us.

I don't really mean to fuse.

Oh, when will I see, the room you have prepared for me.

As I stand my watch, looking for you.

The day, the hour, I have no clue.

Some days you're up, some days you're down. Some days you smile and other days you frown.

Then I find myself crying out when, when, when, when will you come for me

When with you I will be.

Oh to walk the streets of gold as you wipe my tears away

Well done I hope to hear you say.

But until then, I will be watching and waiting

Until you come again.

Amen!

www.ingramcontent.com/pod-product-compliance
Lightning Source LLC
LaVergne TN
LVHW021411080426
835508LV00020B/2549